T0413376

PARROTFISH

by Rachel Rose

BEARPORT
PUBLISHING

Minneapolis, Minnesota

Credits

Cover and title page, © UteNiemann/Adobe Stock; 3, © roc8jas/iStock; 4–5, © Artur_Sarkisyan/Shutterstock; 6, © Griffin/Adobe Stock; 6–7, © Rich Carey/Shutterstock; 9, © cascoly2/Adobe Stock; 10, © ifish/iStock; 11, © mirecca/iStock; 13, © Christian Edelmann/iStock; 15, © Tidewater Teddy/Shutterstock; 17, © CHUYN/iStock; 18–19, © Damsea/Shutterstock; 20–21, © mirecca/iStock; 22T, © stevezmina1/iStock; 22B, © Anastasia Vintovkina/iStock; 23, © cinoby/iStock.

Bearport Publishing Company Product Development Team

President: Jen Jenson; Director of Product Development: Spencer Brinker; Managing Editor: Allison Juda; Associate Editor: Naomi Reich; Associate Editor: Tiana Tran; Art Director: Colin O'Dea; Designer: Kayla Eggert; Product Development Assistant: Owen Hamlin

STATEMENT ON USAGE OF GENERATIVE ARTIFICIAL INTELLIGENCE

Bearport Publishing remains committed to publishing high-quality nonfiction books. Therefore, we restrict the use of generative AI to ensure accuracy of all text and visual components pertaining to a book's subject. See BearportPublishing.com for details.

Library of Congress Cataloging-in-Publication Data is available at www.loc.gov or upon request from the publisher.

ISBN: 979-8-89232-023-8 (hardcover)
ISBN: 979-8-89232-501-1 (paperback)
ISBN: 979-8-89232-148-8 (ebook)

For more information, write to Bearport Publishing, 5357 Penn Avenue South, Minneapolis, MN 55419.

Contents

AWESOME
Parrotfish!

CRUNCH! Deep in the ocean, a colorful parrotfish takes a bite out of some coral. Its powerful beak makes easy work of the hard snack. With their bright bodies and superstrong teeth, parrotfish are awesome!

PARROTFISH GET THEIR NAME BECAUSE OF THEIR BIRDLIKE BEAKS AND PARROTLIKE COLORS.

All Kinds of Everything

There are more than 80 kinds of parrotfish swimming in the sea, and they all look a little different. These fish come in many shapes, sizes, and colors.

As its name suggests, the bumphead parrotfish has a big bump on its head. The stoplight parrotfish is named for its red, green, and yellow coloring.

A stoplight parrotfish

MALE PARROTFISH ARE MORE COLORFUL THAN FEMALES.

A bumphead parrotfish

Tough Teeth

What do all these colorful fish have in common? Their large front teeth! These sharp chompers are **fused** together, making them superstrong—stronger than many metals. The colorful fish even grow extra teeth in their throats! That way, they have new teeth to replace any that fall out.

EACH PARROTFISH HAS ABOUT 1,000 TEETH.

Fused teeth

Crunchy Treats

Parrotfish live in **tropical** coral **reefs** in oceans all around the world. Most of their days are spent feeding on the **algae** inside coral. To get to it, the parrotfish bite off chunks of hard coral. *CHOMP!* Then, the fish grind down the coral with their fused teeth to get to the algae. When parrotfish are done, they poop out the coral—as sand!

A SINGLE PARROTFISH CAN POOP OUT UP TO 2,000 POUNDS (900 KG) OF SAND EVERY YEAR.

Healthy Reefs

Parrotfish not only look good, they're also a big help to their reef **habitats**. Coral can get taken over by dead algae, which stops the reef from growing. By eating the algae, parrotfish make space for new and healthy coral to grow. More healthy coral reefs mean more places for fish and other sea animals to live.

THERE ARE MORE THAN ONE MILLION KINDS OF SEA ANIMALS THAT MAKE THEIR HOMES IN CORAL REEFS.

Bubble Wrap

After chowing down and pooping all day, it's time for sleep. *ZZZ!* Some kinds of parrotfish wrap themselves in a slimy cocoon as they snooze. The clear bubble is made of a goo that comes from their gills. It keeps parasites from biting them while they sleep. The gooey cocoon also hides their smell from **predators**, such as sharks and eels.

PARROTFISH OFTEN SLEEP FOR 10 HOURS AT A TIME.

A cocoon

While sea predators can be a problem for parrotfish, the biggest dangers come from humans. **Pollution** makes their underwater homes unhealthy. Many parrotfish are also overfished, which means too many of them are being taken out of the ocean. Fortunately, there are people trying to help. Some work to take trash out of the water and others pass laws to protect parrotfish.

AS PARROTFISH DISAPPEAR, REEFS SUFFER. THE OTHER SEA ANIMALS THAT LIVE IN THEM DO, TOO.

Time for School

Parrotfish are social animals. They often swim in large groups called schools. The schools are made up of mostly females but are typically led by a male.

When it's time to **mate**, several groups come together. The females lay their eggs in the water, and then the males **fertilize** the floating eggs.

A school of parrotfish

THERE ARE ABOUT 40 PARROTFISH IN A SCHOOL.

Girls and Boys

Once they've been fertilized, it takes about a day for little fish to hatch from the eggs. By the third day, the baby fish begin to feed.

Nearly all parrotfish start their lives out as females. As they grow older, some of the larger females turn into the brightly colored males. The males lead the schools of fish in reefs all around the ocean.

PARROTFISH USUALLY LIVE FOR ABOUT 7 YEARS.

PARROTFISH ARE AWESOME!
LET'S LEARN EVEN MORE ABOUT THEM.

Kind of animal: Parrotfish are fish. Like most fish, they are **cold-blooded** animals that breathe with gills.

Other cold-blooded animals: Fish aren't the only cold-blooded animals. Reptiles and amphibians, such as snakes and frogs, are cold-blooded, too.

Size: Parrotfish can grow up to 4 feet (1 m) long. That's about the same size as a hockey net!

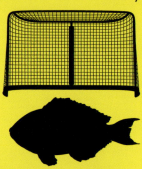

PARROTFISH AROUND THE WORLD

Arctic Ocean

NORTH AMERICA

EUROPE

ASIA

Pacific Ocean

Atlantic Ocean

AFRICA

Pacific Ocean

Indian Ocean

SOUTH AMERICA

AUSTRALIA

N
W E
S

Southern Ocean

Where parrotfish may live

ANTARCTICA

Glossary

algae tiny plantlike living things that grow in water

cold-blooded having a body temperature that rises and drops depending on how much heat the animal gets from its environment

females parrotfish that can lay eggs

fertilize to make an egg able to produce young

fused joined together

habitats places in nature where animals and plants live

male a parrotfish that cannot lay eggs

mate to come together in order to have young

pollution anything that makes something dirty

predators animals that hunt and kill other animals for food

reefs chains of rocks or coral near the water's surface

tropical having to do with the warm areas of Earth near the equator

Index

Read More

Borgert-Spaniol, Megan. *Parrotfish: Coral Reef Cleaners (Animal Eco Influencers)*. Minneapolis: Abdo Publishing, 2020.

Idzikowski, Lisa. *Protecting Ocean Animals (Saving Animals with Science)*. Minneapolis: Lerner Publications, 2024.

Learn More Online

1. Go to **www.factsurfer.com** or scan the QR code below.
2. Enter "**Parrotfish**" into the search box.
3. Click on the cover of this book to see a list of websites.

About the Author

Rachel Rose writes books for kids and teaches yoga. Her favorite animal for all time is her dog, Sandy.